THE ULTIMATE BREATHING WORKOUT

BY: JAIME VENDERA

Vendera
Publishing

ISBN: 978-0-9749411-4-1
Cover Design: Molly Burnside
Illustration: Benoit Guerville
Editor: Amy Chesbro
Contributors: Ryan Murdock, Michael White
Interior Design: Scribe Freelance | www.scribefreelance.com

Machine Gunn Eddie used by permission
Machine Gunn Eddie © 1989
Written by Jim Gillette and Michael Angelo
Published by C U at the Top Music, Inc. (ASCAP)

Other books by the author:
Raise Your Voice
The Ultimate Vocal Workout Diary
Mindset: Programming Your Mind for Success
*The 11 Secret Steps to Writing, Designing, Creating
& Self-Publishing Your Very Own "How To" Book, eBook or Manual*

CONTENTS

CONTENTS

SPECIAL NOTE!
To Access the audio files, go to
http://www.thevoiceconnection.com/breathefree.html

This book is dedicated to
My beautiful wife
My Eternal Soul mate

DIANE VENDERA

You Breathed
Life into Me

The power of the voice is astounding. You possess the most powerful, individually unique instrument ever created. The power of the voice can command the attention of thousands and exhilarate a nation. The voice can invoke every single emotion imaginable; it can revitalize the soul or it can bring a person to tears. But, the intense energy of the voice cannot be brought to life without the initial spark . . . the breath. . . .

The breath can give life to a singer's voice and it can as easily take it away. It truly depends on each individual singer's understanding and interpretation of correct breath technique and the interpretations have been many. How can something as simplistic as simply breathing be quite so misunderstood? That's what I decided to find out. . . .

When I first wrote *Raise Your Voice*, I had written what I considered the most completely developed and informative vocal training manual I could ever possibly want. Since that time, I have spent countless hours studying vocal techniques.

I still continue to search for new material each and every day to improve my teaching skills, to expand my vocal expertise. Some areas of my expertise I took for granted; breath support for instance. . . .

I have been blessed with the ability to sustain notes for what has seemed like an eternity. Whenever I used to perform, I was always asked the same question by aspiring singers: "How do you hold out your notes that long?" I always have the same response; "I practice my own training methods and if you'd follow my vocal training program from my book, *Raise Your Voice*, you could achieve these same results." Although I stand by the breath training methods in *Raise Your Voice*, I have re-discovered a series of exercises guaranteed to help improve your breathing and breath support; thus this book was created.

These exercises have helped to build my vocal power, stamina and breath release and I have even had students who have used these exercises as a relief for asthma, although I am not a doctor and can in no way verify this fact.

But I can verify the results I have seen in breathing improvement from this system. So I have to ask you the following question. "How would you like to sustain your notes for thirty seconds or longer?" Do I have your attention?

If you are a fan of my website for singers, The Voice Connection, then you probably already knew that I studied vocal technique at The Vocal Institute of Technology at the Musician's Institute, in Hollywood California. Let me share with you an important story from my time at M.I.

One day as I was skimming through my old V.I.T. notebooks, I stumbled across a breathing program that I had totally forgotten about. This simple program was presented to me during one of my vocal lessons at M.I. by my vocal coach **Bryan Kelly; Bryan** was one of several vocal teachers from V.I.T. **Bryan** is the brother of the late **Tim Kelly**, former guitarist of the band **Slaughter**.

Bryan had told me that the set of breathing exercises from the program were rumored to be the breathing exercises that **Geoff Tate**, lead singer of **Queensryche**, had used to help develop his incredible voice. I have yet to find out if this is true, but if you listen to the beginning of the song, "**Queen of the Ryche**", you'll know that if it is true, it definitely worked!

This breathing program originally consisted of four specific exercises. I played around with the program for a few weeks, but, due to my curiosity towards perfection, I expanded on the basic premise of the exercises and turned this simple four-exercise set into a full blown nine step breathing workout!

GET READY TO BREATHE!

Are you ready to take the **Vendera Breathing Challenge**? I dare you – no, I double dare you to try this program for ninety days and chart your progress, like I originally did over fifteen years ago. I can almost promise you that your sustain time will double, possibly even triple in length. Not only will your breath capacity increase, but your voice will become stronger as well and the quality of your voice will improve.

How is this possible? How in the world could the voice possibly improve in quality just through performing simple breathing exercises and developing correct breath technique?

The answer is simple: By developing proper breath technique, the quality of your voice will dramatically improve because using less breath means less force on the cords. Less force on the vocal cords means producing each tone more efficiently with less effort. Less effort means allowing more resonance to be produced for a richer, fuller tone. More resonance means minimization of vocal strain. Minimization of vocal strain means a long-lived career. Get the picture?

Now let me stop right here and tell you that breathing exercises by themselves WILL NOT improve your singing voice! You will NOT become a better singer just by doing breathing exercises. Singing and vocal exercises are what help develop the voice. Practicing technical vocal exercises, learning to apply correct singing technique and singing every day are the tools for developing a great voice. But, by adding these exercises to your regular vocal regimen, you WILL develop better, stronger, more efficient breathing habits, which will cross over into a stronger singing voice!

Still, I must state that it is my belief that correct breathing is the foundation of a strong and healthy voice. So let's quit wasting time and get on with the show.

THE BASICS

Before we delve into the exercises, I think we all need a refresher course in Breathing 101. Do you know the correct way to breathe as applied to singing? Do you consider your self an excellent breather? Let's find out.

You must sing from your diaphragm, tighten your stomach, raise your chest, push your stomach out, suck your stomach in, tighten your butt cheeks, push the entire breath out . . . I've heard kazillions of explanations on how a singer should breathe, and tried too many outrageous breathing methods to mention. It's enough to drive you nuts. I think it did drive me nuts. But facts are facts . . . Breathing is a natural function and should be naturally effortless!

The main objective of this program is to help you develop naturally correct breathing techniques which are required to support the singer's voice, especially rock singers. If you develop correct technique, you'll learn that both low notes and high notes require very little breath to sustain them.

You'll develop the breath control needed to prevent you from singing too breathy or pushing too hard, and you'll eliminate the vocal strain that's associated with poor breathing habits. Are you ready to learn? You better pay attention. . . .

I want you to first start by looking at yourself in a full sized mirror where you can study your physical reactions as you try this first exercise. Okay, are you looking at yourself in the mirror? Are you ready? Do you want me to shut up? All right, all ready! Here we go.

As you are watching yourself in the mirror, I want you to take the biggest and deepest breath that you can, as quickly as you can. Now tell me what physically changed? You *were* watching yourself, right? Try it one more time, but this time, pay closer attention.

Did you happen to notice any part of your body moving? What moved? Did your shoulders rise up? Did your stomach go out or in? Was it expanding or contracting? Did your chest expand? Did your ribs or back expand? Did your neck tighten up or your neck muscles bulge out?

These are all good questions to ask yourself as you inhale. Now, I know I wasn't there looking in the mirror with you, but I'll lay money down that at least seventy-five percent of each and every one of you allowed your shoulders to raise until your neck disappeared and expanded your chest until you looked like a puffer kite. What's wrong with this? EVERYTHING! This is the #1 totally incorrect way for singers to breathe. Unfortunately, it is the breathing pattern that the majority of us have developed out of habit.

This book is a guide to both improving your breathing for singing and life in general, so right this instant, I want you to stop, put the book down and go to breathing.com and click on the breathing test link. Take the breathing test to see where you fall among the ranks of natural breathers.

You'll notice that there are many other products on these sites devoted to breathing. These products were created by a friend of mine, Michael White. Feel free to explore these other books and products on breathing as I am positive that you will feel the need to check them out even further after you finish this book. After all, breath is life, so I encourage you to learn as much as you can about breathing.

Now that you've taken the breathing test, which was created by breathing specialist, **Michael Grant White**, I would like for him to personally explain the true path to natural every day breathing, because breathing is life. I want you to find your way back to naturally effortless breathing and I believe Mike has the perfect way to explain it:

SUPPORTING A MORE OPTIMAL BREATHING PATTERN: THE PEAR + THE CONE = THE WAVE

An optimal deep breath starts with an inhalation that is fuller and slower. As the diaphragm flattens, the lower torso expands in all directions (70%), then the ribs and chest expand (30%), engaging the entire torso in an upward wave-like motion. This is followed by the relaxed exhalation, and then a pause. . . .

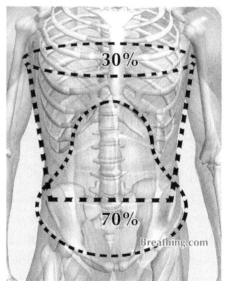

Inhale (lungs full)

THE PEAR . . .

Imagine a pear hanging from your collarbones. Your diaphragm lies on top of the lower, round portion of the pear, and rises and falls with each breath. At the end of an exhale, the diaphragm rests up inside your ribs in its natural, dome shape. During an inhale, as your lungs fill, the top of the pear is pushed down and the

13

diaphragm flattens. This causes the lower, round part of the pear (stomach, liver, intestines) to expand outward in 360 degrees.

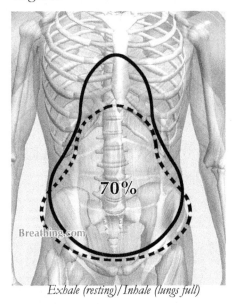

70%

Breathing.com

Exhale (resting)/Inhale (lungs full)

The soft tissue of the abdomen will expand more than the sides (intercostal muscles) and more than your lower back and kidney areas, but you should still feel expansion in your sides and back—although you may not, due to low-back tension. This primary pear movement should account for about 70% of the volume of your in-breath, since most of your lung tissue is in the lower half of your torso. Indeed, the lungs hang down about 20% more in the back like the tails on a tuxedo).

THE CONE

After the pear is filled, the breath will naturally rise up to open the ribs and expand the chest. This is the secondary movement of the inhale, which accounts for about 30% of its volume. Imagine a cone with the point anchored at your navel. The upper circle of the cone is approximately at your nipples. First the pear, then the cone enlarge in a wave-like movement upward. The ribs expand after the lungs need more space for a deeper breath. The circle of the cone opens wider as the ribs spread sideways—but not upward.

The cone is anchored at the navel. It will expand at the bottom, but not lose its foundation. If the ribs were lifted upward during an inhale by shrugging the shoulders or bulging the neck muscles, the circle at the top of the cone might even decrease in diameter, restricting your air volume intake. Tension would accumulate from doing shoulder shrugs and tensing the neck muscles about 18,000 times a day! This could lead to "high-chest dominant" or "reverse breathing," where the abdomen GOES IN during an inhale. The ideal is to keep your shoulders and

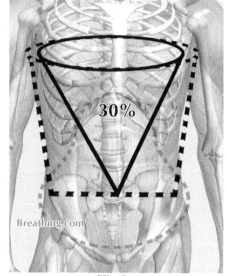

The Cone

neck at rest and allow your ribs to widen sideways. There can be a gentle rippling movement in the shoulders and neck muscles as the inhale peaks.

THE WAVE

The merging of the pear and cone as one continuous movement creates a marvelous wave that first fills the belly, then rises into the thorax. You can harmonize the breath wave with the spinal wave. The gentle undulation of the spine will encourage the flow of spinal fluid, lubricating your spinal discs. Since the majority of your activity and attention should be in your lower torso, you will be stimu-

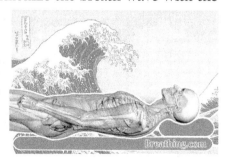

The Wave

lating the vagus nerve and the parasympathetic (calming) side of your autonomic nervous system. Like an ocean wave, when your inhale comes to its peak, it will spill its momentum on the shore, with your free and relaxed exhale. You may feel inclined to pause before your next inhale, because you will be oxygenated and refreshed.

THE SQUEEZE & BREATHE EXERCISE

To strengthen the dia-phragm from within, per-form the breath wave while placing a little extra pressure with your hands in the soft tissue between your hips and your ribs. Place your four fingers in the front and your thumbs in the back over your kidneys. Do this while standing with your feet shoulder-width apart, knees slightly bent, chin raised slightly above the horizon

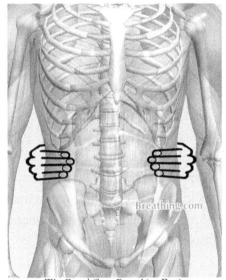

The Pear/Cone Breathing Ratio

level. Breathe out all the way while squeezing in. Now hold these "vises" tightly while you inhale. As your "lower pear" expands, you are exercising your diaphragm muscle. Your fingers and thumbs will be slowly forced open. Do this six to ten times, with a 4-count inhale and a 6-to-8-count exhale. Take a regular breath in between each squeeze to give yourself a rest, to feel the flush of blood to this area, and to note any other changes.

Any dizziness suggests a low tolerance for energy. If dizzy, wait 30–60 seconds before doing more in order to give your body a chance to absorb the excess energy. When practiced regularly over time, this exercise can improve your diaphragmatic action and increase your lung volume. More advanced breathing techniques are available at: www.breathing .com.

No breathing pattern is static, but experience has shown that a good pattern should have a strong tendency toward this 70/30 ratio, due to the sufficient support needed by one's internal core—also known as the dan tien, the hara, or the internal foundation—which includes the diaphragm. This ratio promotes "rest, digest & heal."

The 70/30 ratio may change dramatically—even to its opposite of 30/70—when the system encounters extreme degrees of stress or distress, "fight or fight." By consciously directing your breath, you can gently and consciously bring your breathing back to the 70/30 balance to better manage and recover from distress.

In the #176 Breathing Development Fundamentals program [Breathing.com], this area is called "the bottom of the pear." We also liken it to the "basement" of an office building, with the "building" being the lungs, and the "elevator" being the diaphragm and wave-like movement that rises and descends with the breath.

From Michael Grant White, Optimal Breathing® and Breathing.com. Copyright © Michael Grant White 2006, 2008. All rights reserved. As published in *Heal Yourself with Breath, Light, Sound & Water* by Denis Ouellette.

Mike is a somatic educator using the breath as a focal point for stress management, emotional balance, self expression, optimum health and personal power. As a health educator, personal growth mentor, author, breathing development specialist, public speaker, & vocalist Mike has successfully helped thousands transform their lives through better breathing, attitudinal healing and nutrition.

He is founder and director of The Optimal Breathing School and www.breathing.com. His original goal was to regain his singing voice. This took over 20 years due to abuse and trauma as a battered child. During that time he learned what did not work and of the need for a common generic approach to breathing just for the sake of breathing, that would aid all approaches to optimum health, peak performance, life extension and spiritual expression. He has combined key elements of Eastern and Western spirituality, Tibetan, Hatha, and Kundalini yogas, pranayama, chi kung (Qigong), massage and bodywork therapy, meditations, tai chi, karate, Reichian Therapy, Radiance Breathwork®, meditation, chanting, toning, operatic and public speaking training, and nutrition. He is a member of the American Holistic Medical Association; American Holistic Health Association and a founding member of Association Of Humanistic Psychology Somatics Community. Mike has been studying the breath and breathing since 1975 and uses his Optimal Breathing Kit, manual, seminar videos and recorded breathing exercises to support his work.

So I am assuming that each and every one of you has taken the breathing test by now, especially now that you've read Mike's great explanation of natural breathing. It is important that you fully understand that the natural way to breathe is by allowing our abdomen, mid and lower back and floating ribs (the lower and side ribs) to expand outward, all around our midsection in 360° and THEN and ONLY then, allow the upper chest to expand. This is an outward expansion of the ribs, not an upwards expansion which is evident from a lifting up of the shoulders. A shoulder lift only causes stress. This is where Mike's "Squeeze and Breathe" would come into play to make sure you are breathing correctly.

For singers, breathing begins at the bottom and works its way up the body; starting at the belly then moving upwards. Actually it is probably more simultaneous, but by focusing on the bottom (belly below the navel and back) I am assured that you will master this process. If the chest expands, as long as it is last in line, that is fine. In fact, Mike promotes healthy chest expansion and as I stated in the last paragraph, it is part of natural breathing.

But, when referring to singing, I am adamant about keeping you away from chest breathing. Why? Because this is where singers fall short with breath support. By totally breathing high in the upper front of the chest, a singer will prevent the lungs from filling up completely and add strain to the voice and neck area. Natural breathing is about the entire process and healthy rib expansion for full intake, whereas singing is about full expansion without locking in the upper chest. Besides, I don't really think you'll need a full breath up through the chest in order to sustain your notes. (I do take full bottom to top breaths for breaking glasses though.)

This is why I say that you can expand the upper chest as long as it is last in line. It is better to first develop your lower belly breathing. It is the way GOD intended it. Just watch a baby breathing while lying in a crib. Notice how their little bellies rise up and down with every breath they take. To totally understand the relevance of the baby breath please go to: www.breathing.com/articles/baby-belly breath.htm

For fun, let's try it ourselves. No, I don't want you climbing into a crib. I want you to lie down on the floor, flat on your back and slowly breathe in through your nose and out through your mouth. (Mouth breathing without any controlled force such as with speaking or singing may invite snoring.) As you breathe in through your nose, concentrate on making your stomach rise.

If you are having trouble making your stomach rise, try putting a large book on your stomach and focus on making it rise each time you inhale and allowing the book to drop back down as the stomach flattens on the exhale. If you have trouble with the book sliding off your stomach, try using a sack of sugar, rice or sand bag from a yoga props store. (Thanks for that tip, Mike.) See how easy that was? Now stand up and try it again. It's not as easy when you aren't lying on the ground; is it?

Re-learning to breathe correctly through natural lower abdominal breathing takes a little time getting used to, but you will get the hang of it. If you stick to the program, in a short amount of time, it will become second nature.

WHAT WORKS WHERE?

For years, a lot of teachers have preached the praises of diaphragmatic breathing, but do you really have any clue what they have been talking about? I know that I didn't! Every time my first teacher said, "breathe from the diaphragm", I just assumed I had to make it happen and had to put a LOT of tension into my mid-section. Wrong answer!

So let's start on the right path by learning a "correct" thing or two about breathing anatomy. When you inhale, the air flows into the mouth, down the trachea, (more commonly called the throat or pharynx) and into the lungs. What makes the process easier is that muscle that we've all heard about one zillion times during the course of singing instruction- the diaphragm.

The diaphragm is a large dome-shaped muscle at the bottom of the ribs that separates the body in half. The TRUE purpose of the diaphragm is to create a vacuum in the lungs to allow the lungs to draw in air for equalization of air pressure.

When you inhale, the diaphragm flattens out by expanding downward towards the stomach, making more room for the lungs to expand. (This is why the stomach expands outward. The stomach has no choice but to make room for the diaphragm. Thus, the "book on the belly" exercise you've already performed is to teach you to expand the diaphragm.)

If you don't engage the diaphragm, you are preventing the lungs from expanding to their maximum capacity. If you are a fan of my book, *Raise Your Voice*, you'll know that I use the visual of the lungs filling with air from the bottom-up. This is to get the singer used to that lower belly breath sensation. In all actuality, the lungs are more like a balloon. Balloons fill up due to the shape that FORMS them from the outside. That is exactly why the belly most often expands more than the ribs.

This can only happen if the lungs have room to expand. That's why the floating ribs should expand outwards. It's easy to tell if you are using your diaphragm when you inhale, because your stomach will expand due to the diaphragm dropping. Remember how little baby's bellies expand?

When you allow your stomach to expand first as opposed to your upper chest, you are allowing the diaphragm to properly expand and thus maximizing your lung expansion by making more room in the chest cavity.

"So what if only my chest expands instead of my stomach?" That's fine if you are only planning on being a mediocre breather, asthmatic or a mediocre singer, for that matter. That's your choice.

Chest breathing would be similar to only filling about one-third of a vase with water. When you breathe in by engaging your diaphragm, you'll fill at least two-thirds of your lungs with air (or 2/3 of the vase with water). Which type of breathing seems the better choice for sustaining long notes? This is an easy question.

_____

Note: The belly isn't really filling with air; it just expands because of the diaphragm contractions.

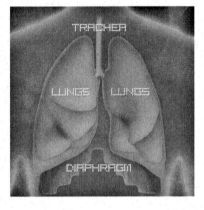

"If the diaphragm helps the inhalation process, why do so many teachers preach to sing from the diaphragm as I am singing?" They have been taught that the diaphragm is respon- sible for breath support. Are they wrong? Not totally. I believe that a lot of teachers just don't fully understand the diaphragm because of years of misinformation. The diaphragm is only partially responsible for breath support.

So what part does the diaphragm play in the role of breath support? The diaphragm's main role is handling the inhalation cycle of breathing. However, diaphragm involvement in breath support comes into play when the diaphragm is "allowed" to relax back to its normal position without excess stress placed upon it from muscles such as the abdominal muscles.

No stress on the diaphragm means the vacuum is maintained for a longer period of time within the lungs, which slows the release of air. This process can be further assisted by using a technique that I call the **Inhalation Sensation**. You'll better understand this term at the end of the book when I teach you the secrets of breathing. So, as far as singing is concerned, what's responsible for the exhalation cycle? The stomach and back muscles are the main responsible parties.

When you exhale, the abdominal and back muscles should slightly tighten to slightly nudge the diaphragm along as it relaxes to return to its neutral position. This nudging is what gives singers control of breath release and increased volume/power.

This tightening is more noticeable when singing; in some cases, too noticeable. Too many singers incorrectly over-tighten the stomach when singing. This causes excess strain on the diaphragm and forces a rushed release of air from the lungs, which could possibly lead to vocal strain. There is a correct way to tighten the stomach without hurting your voice. You'll learn about that at the end of the book too. Enough about that. Now back to the exhalation process.

When the diaphragm starts to return to its normal position, air is released from the lungs. You can control the rate of air release by adjusting the amount of stomach muscle tension. If you'd like to know what this should feel like for a singer, take a deep breath, then pretend that you are quickly blowing out a candle flame.

Another example is to hiss like you were a hose letting off pressure. Did you feel your stomach tighten and then relax? This is stomach (abdominal) and back muscle tension. (Please note that when I am referring to stomach muscle tension, I am collectively referring to both the abdominal and back muscles, because they both work together for support.)

When singing, you must learn to adjust the amount of stomach muscle tension so as not to force the air release from the lungs too quickly.

If you incorrectly over-tighten the stomach muscles or push

too hard, you won't be able to sustain notes for very long, because you'll deplete your air supply very rapidly. This air supply is the fuel that vibrates your vocal cords.

If you use too much breath pressure, you'll also dry out your vocal cords, which can create vocal strain because the cords resist this air pressure in order to vibrate. Too much air leads to breathy, non-resonant tones that aggravate the vocal cords; so our goal is to master our breath release.

The breath support (stomach/back muscle) tension that you want to feel when singing is minute (unless you are an opera or rock singer). You should maintain the slightly tense feeling in your stomach that you had felt when you were pretending to blow out a candle, but without completely locking your stomach. If you haven't developed your breath technique and you lock the stomach, you could unconsciously lock at your throat, like grunting, which will cause vocal strain. That exact amount of back/stomach muscle tension you want to master for breath support is "firm but flexible" but constantly there.

"So how do I know if my stomach muscles are too tight?" Try this little experiment. Put your hand on your stomach and grunt. Did you feel your stomach muscles and throat lock? This is way too tight for singing, unless you know how to do it properly. NEVER grunt when you are singing or speaking for that matter.

Whenever you grunt, you simultaneously tighten the abdominal wall, back muscles and throat muscles and slam shut the vocal cords. This can be vocally damaging, because now you have a build up of excess breath pressure trying to escape through a closed valve. When you are singing, you should have a slight tension in the stomach.

In other words, if someone socked you in the gut, the air should fly right out. I hope that doesn't happen, but you get the picture. Just remember this saying. "**Firm but Flexible.**" The stomach muscles should always feel firm, but should also be flexible to touch.

Note: When applying Power Push support for singing rock music, the stomach *will* be rock solid. You'll learn about the Power Push at the end of the book.

MAXIMUM BREATH POTENTIAL

Okay, what have we learned so far about the breathing process? You open your mouth and inhale. Your diaphragm should drop which causes the stomach to bulge out to make room for the diaphragm. This, in turn, makes room for the lungs to fully expand by creating a vacuum within the lungs to draw in air. Then, when you sing, maintain that "firm but flexible" tension in the stomach muscles.

I'm assuming that you will now be faithfully practicing diaphragmatic breathing. It's simple. Inhale. Expand the belly, and keep the shoulders down. I know that at first it seems difficult to get used to breathing like this all of the time, but it gets easier. How else are you going to completely fill up the lungs?

Oh, wait a minute, did I say completely? I thought that I said diaphragmatic breathing only fills up two-thirds of the lungs? All right, you caught me. There is another way to breathe that allows you to COMPLETELY fill up the lungs if you wish to do so. It's called **lower abdominal breathing** or what I refer to as using your **Maximum Breath Potential**. (You really already know this as Mike explained it quite well.)

The best way that I have found for singers to utilize a natural breathing pattern is combining both diaphragmatic and chest breathing into one process by focusing on breathing first below the navel.

"How do I combine the two types of breathing?" Glad you asked. Let's try yet another exercise. Remember the vase? When you pour water into a vase, it completely fills from the bottom-up. Imagine your body as the vase; fill your body with air, just as if you were filling a vase with water. Take a deep breath in through your nose and allow your stomach to begin expanding all the way down below the belly button (navel).

Remember, you are a vase, so I expect your back muscles and ribs to expand as well. A vase doesn't fill up on just one side; it fills up in 360° around the vase. You should visualize air filling up your entire lower body in 360°, expanding your stomach, sides and back. After your stomach expands, keep filling up your vase with air, working up towards the ribs.

Allow your ribs to fully expand as if they were opening up like a flower. One crucial aspect of breathing that most of my earlier vocal teachers failed to mention was rib and back expansion. Always allow expansion of the back and ribs when you inhale. This expansion involves the *intercostal muscles*.

The intercostal muscles are situated in between the ribs. The contraction of the intercostals will pull the ribs upward and outward, resulting in chest expansion. The more room you create in the chest area, the more room you are creating for lung expansion.

Towards the last draw of your breath before you are

completely full of air, you must allow your upper chest to begin expanding outwards, not upwards. I bet by the time you are finished, you'll be full of more hot air than you've ever imagined!

Before moving on, I must say that I can't truly think of a time that I had to fill my lungs to this extent, but if I ever needed to, I most definitely could. (Actually, I do use a complete full breath for my glass shattering gigs.)

You really don't need a huge amount of air to sustain long notes. You should be able to sustain high, low, loud, or soft notes with the smallest amount of air. It's all about mastering the release of air through breath control.

"So, then why is **Maximum Breath Potential** so beneficial to a singer?" Because like I said, learning to sustain longer notes is about breath control and developing an efficient, consistent breathing machine. If you work to develop your maximum inhalation and maximum exhalation, you will have developed and strengthened your breathing apparatus to its fullest extent, enabling you to maintain total breath control with greater ease. You will develop the ultimate breathing machine . . . YOU!

It's just like weight lifting. If you start with bicep curls with ten pound weights and in a few weeks move up to twenty pound weights, you can do ten pound curls much easier because you have worked beyond that level. You have reached a higher plateau. This program is about working beyond your highest level; reaching a higher plateau so that when you sing your breath machine is much stronger than needed and then you can give it your all with minimized effort.

By developing your lung capacity through this type of

breathing, you'll strengthen your entire breathing mechanism. The more room you create for lung capacity, the less air you'll need in order to sustain long notes. The stronger the entire breathing mechanism becomes, (lungs, diaphragm, intercostal, back and stomach muscles) the less the machine has to work to be efficient.

Like I said, it's like lifting weights. If you begin working out with fifty pounds of weight, over time you'll gain muscle and increase your strength. You'll eventually have to increase your weight, say, to one hundred pounds. Now, fifty pounds is suddenly easier, right?

So in conclusion, if you want to become an ultimate breathing machine, you must first learn to breathe properly. This means you must switch your breathing patterns from chest breathing to diaphragmatic breathing, and then add in lower abdominal breathing.

"And how do I do this?" By learning to engage the diaphragm and intercostals to expand your belly and back muscles. This type of breathing should become a way of life for you. I can't put it any simpler; CHANGE THE WAY YOU BREATHE! Period! Simply put, expand your lung capacity by developing lower abdominal breathing and rib expansion or your **Maximum Breath Potential**. Do I need to repeat myself? Expand the stomach, back, ribs, and finally, expand the chest.

Three little secrets to developing a natural breathing pattern are:

1. The book on the belly exercise.
2. Placing your hands on your sides and feeling the ribs expand as you breathe.

3. Mentally focusing on filling the vase, by first expanding from the belly below the navel, then working up towards the chest.

These can actually be practiced as three separate beginning exercises. Simply do three sets of 20-30 repetitions of inhaling/exhaling with each exercise. If you'd do this for a minimum of two weeks, you will start to adopt a natural breathing pattern.

All right, I am assuming that you put this book down for the last two weeks and busted your butt on the three-exercise program. If you got a little bored and went to breathing.com to do a little breathing research, that's fine. I am glad that you are all curious students. Now let's get back to work. The next step is to learn how to control the breath flow, or in other words the rate of air release from the lungs, also known as breath support. Breath support is the key to a singer's success and the premise of this book.

"So how am I going to accomplish this", you ask? Don't worry. I've got you covered. The following nine-exercise system will show you how to maximize your breathing potential and lead you towards developing the ultimate vocal machine:

DISCLAIMER: The following sections are not intended to prescribe, treat, prevent or diagnose any illness. Please consult your physician before attempting any of the following exercises. The author is in no way responsible for your health and/or success.

THE ROUTINE

Before we begin the exercises, I suggest that you purchase a stopwatch for tracking your time. You can purchase one from any sports store or a family shopping store like K-Mart. Stopwatches vary in price from $10.00-$100.00. You don't need anything fancy, a basic stopwatch will do. If you are an iPhone user, you could also purchase a stopwatch from the aps store.

If you are a computer nerd, like me, you can also use my software program, the *Vendera Digital Vocal Coach.* It has everything you'd ever need for vocal training- stopwatch, tuner, metronome, volume meter, tone generator, vocal scale generator, digital recorder. . . . Yes, I am shamelessly promoting another one of my other products, haha.

You'll be writing down your sustain times to keep track of your progress. You can write these down in any notebook or you can record the data in *The Ultimate Vocal Workout Diary;* a diary for users of my methods to keep precise records of their progress.

The following exercises should be followed in the exact order presented. They were designed to develop correct breathing technique in three steps. The first step will to teach you how to breathe properly. The second step will help you strengthen the lungs, diaphragm, intercostal, stomach and back muscles. The third step will develop breath control and increase your breath release/sustain time.

Before we get started, I want you to grab a piece of paper

and write down the names of the following exercises:

Abdominal Release #1-
Abdominal Release #2-
Breath Capacity #1-
Breath Capacity #2-
Breath Release #1-
Breath Release #2-
Sustain #1-
Sustain #2-
Sustain #3-

The reason I had you write down the names of the exercises, is because you really do need to begin keeping a journal of your daily progress, so that you can follow along with the program and review how well you are improving. (Again, *The Ultimate Vocal Workout Diary* has the names of the exercises already laid out in weekly chart form.)

Each and every week, I want you to review your "breathing journal" to decide which areas need improving and which areas are developing at a steady rate. If you practice this series faithfully for at least three months, you'll be ready for the breathing Olympics!

So are you ready to get started? Here we go!

ABDOMINAL RELEASE #1

The first exercise in this series will strengthen the abdominal muscles and intercostals, while focusing on developing your **Maximum Breath Potential**. In **The Basics**, I explained to you how you must maintain a tensing in the stomach muscles as if you were blowing out a candle. This exercise focuses on that same sensation as you are hissing. By hissing the air out, you'll strengthen the abdominal and back muscles.

Start by taking a deep breath in through the nose. Remember to breathe into your belly first, focusing below the navel. (Remember, this is just a visual. The air isn't *really* going into the stomach.) Make sure to fill the vase from the bottom up. Don't forget to expand the ribs by engaging the intercostals.

Begin by hissing a sustained "sssss". Let's try it again, but set your stopwatch first and begin to hiss at a steady, controlled rate.

There will come a point when your stomach muscles begin to burn. It will feel uncomfortable and a little funny, like you aren't in control of your stomach or breathing. Try to hang on. It's going to be very tempting to give up and inhale, but **don't do it**. Just think; the longer you are able to hang on, the closer you are coming to sustaining notes with ease for longer periods of time and developing a seemingly unlimited breathing power. You are developing stomach muscle control.

ABDOMINAL RELEASE #1 EXAMPLE

The tricky part is keeping the ribs expanded outward for as long as you can. Remember, this exercise is to help strengthen the intercostals as well. If you keep the ribs expanded while you release your air supply, you'll maintain a larger cavity in the chest, which in turn, slows the air release rate.

Your abdominals will basically be fighting your intercostals for control. Your abdominal will want to push in, while your intercostals want to try to stay expanded (although they want to let the ribs collapse when they should stay expanded). Hang tough; don't let your abs win!

You are teaching the abdominal and intercostals a muscle memory pattern or as I prefer to say, you are teaching them patience. They are learning to work together to release breath at a controlled rate. The burning sensation will eventually pass as you strengthen the stomach muscles.

Don't get discouraged if you can't hold out for very long. Ten seconds is fine for your first time. I want you to write down your time on your chart. I'll pretend that I'm doing the process with you for my very first time. I'll use my original progress sheet. My first time, I was able to hang on for thirty-one seconds, but I had already been singing for some time. So, I'll write down the following:

ABDOMINAL RELEASE #1- 31 SECONDS

ABDOMINAL RELEASE #2

Another exercise for strengthening the stomach muscles is to repetitively force your air supply to release on a single breath until you feel that you have completely emptied the lungs. This exercise strengthens both the stomach muscles and lungs.

Start by breathing in through your nose and then completely exhaling by hissing all of the air out. This isn't a slow sustained hiss. I want you to forcefully hiss the air out. This shouldn't take any longer than one second. Hold this empty feeling for about one second and then without inhaling any more air, forcefully exhale again.

Although you'll probably feel like you've completely

expelled your air supply, there is still some oxygen left in the lungs. Our goal is to squish it all out. Exhale at one-second intervals, as many times as you can, on one breath, until you feel you are completely empty of air.

ABDOMINAL RELEASE #2 EXAMPLE

"Why should I put so much emphasis on developing the abdominal muscles if I'm trying to decrease stomach muscle tension?" Because, although typically you don't really need much stomach muscle pressure for singing, a strong set of abs will help you to control "over-tensing" your stomach. AND, you'll have the abdominal strength for a Power Push.

The main culprit of vocal strain and the inability to sustain notes is **incorrectly** "over-tensing" the stomach muscles. (I'll eventually show you how to correctly tighten your stomach muscles for more power ala Power Push, so a strong set of abs is a benefit.)

One might think, "My stomach muscles are too strong, that's why I push so hard." That's not true. Over pushing is actually a sign of untrained or weak muscles and/or an untrained breather.

So, how many times were you able to exhale? I bet that you learned that you have more breath stored in those little lungs than you thought. The lungs aren't used to being emptied to such an extreme. There is usually a tiny bit of air left in the bottom. When you do this exercise, you will release that last bit of stale air trapped in your lungs, which will allow you to inhale a full fresh breath. Trust me, fresh air is a body benefit! A flood of fresh oxygen into the blood stream will boost your energy and metabolism.

Again, the main purpose of this exercise is to strengthen the stomach muscles and lungs. Now I want you to write down how many times you were able to repeat the process. I didn't fair to well my first go at this one. But we all have to start somewhere. I am going to write down that I was able to release and hold two times:

ABDOMINAL RELEASE #2- 2X

BREATH CAPACITY #1

If you want to learn how to sustain longer notes you must learn to control the breath release of your breath capacity. The last two exercises strengthened the intercostals muscles, the back muscles, the abdominal (stomach) muscles, and worked with the lungs, while giving you the chance to practice developing your **Maximum Breath Potential.**

This next exercise works in combination with the lungs and diaphragm, by developing your breath capacity. The longer you can hold your breath, the more comfortable it will be to release air at a slow, controlled rate, without feeling like you are suffocating.

Start by taking a deep belly breath in through your nose and all the way down below your navel, and then hold. Always visualize filling your lungs from the bottom up. Keep your ribs expanded! Set your stopwatch and hold, hold, hold. So, how long can you hold your breath? Remember, the longer you can hold your breath, the closer you are coming to reaching your breathing goals.

You'll get that same muscle burn sensation in the chest and

stomach as you did in the first exercise. That's great! That is a sure sign that this exercise is working. Hold your breath as long as you can. Write down your time on your chart. I was able to hold my breath for forty-four seconds, so I'll write down the following:

BREATH CAPACITY #1- 44 SECONDS

BREATH CAPACITY #2

This time we are going to do the reverse by completely exhaling, then holding our breath on empty. Not only is it beneficial to increase the time you can hold your breath, it is equally important to increase the time you can hold without any breath. Why? Because, this will get you used to the uneasy feeling of slow breath release. By developing your "non-breath" capacity, you'll be prepared for the next few exercises, where we are going to be working on developing your breath control, or your breath release.

You must strengthen the lungs for both full capacity and non-capacity. This way, you will feel comfortable when slowing down the release rate from the lungs. It feels a lot different holding absolutely no breath as opposed to holding a full breath, so be prepared.

As you release your air supply when singing, you get closer and closer to an empty set of lungs. This is when most singers begin to feel uncomfortable and generally let go and give up, even with over half their air supply still left in the lungs.

If you master the breath capacity exercises, you will be prepared to handle any uncomfortable breath release sensation. You'll strengthen the lungs and develop a tolerance for the feeling of an empty set of lungs, so you'll have a better chance of holding on, instead of letting go.

Now get ready to set your stopwatch. Ready, set, exhale and hold as long as you can. I know it's burning and feels pretty uncomfortable, but you are tougher than that. You are hardened steel! Don't give up. . . . Congratulations, you did it! Now, don't you feel good about yourself? I do. I made it for twenty-five seconds so I'll write:

BREATH CAPACITY #2- 25 SECONDS

BREATH RELEASE #1

Time for a new set of exercises . . . the breath release exercises. The true purpose of *The Ultimate Breathing Workout* is to develop your maximum breathing potential. The only way to develop this potential to its fullest is by learning to control breath release by sustaining notes. In the first exercise, **Abdominal Release #1**, you hissed, which was a non-vocal exercise. What I mean by non-vocal is that you weren't making any sound with the vocal cords.

Talking and singing changes everything, as far as breathing is concerned. You are now involving the vocal cords, which resist the air release from the lungs by coming together. This created resistance is what vibrates the vocal cords; as the air is released, it moves between the glottal opening (area between the cords) causing the vocal cords to vibrate together as they resist the air pressure. When you hiss, there is no vocal cord resistance to slow down the release because the glottis is wide open and not trying to resist the breath flow (*abduction*); only when we speak or sing do the cords come together to resist the air pressure. This is called *adduction*.

I know what you are thinking. "If the vocal cords resist the flow of air, then I should be able to hold out notes longer than I can hiss."

Although this sounds like a logical argument, this isn't necessarily so. When you are hissing, you are developing your ability to control the airflow release at a constant rate by adjusting intercostals muscles, diaphragm and stomach muscle pressure, while using the mouth as a pressure release valve.

When you sing, you are involving the work of various vocal muscles and different mouth positions by singing vowels and consonants, which will cause you to lose your breath at variable rates.

Plus, vocal cord vibration is the production of energy. The air is the fuel and the cords are converting that fuel to sound. What happens when you use fuel? You use it up quickly depending on the situation.

When you sing, you are creating sound, so it makes sense to practice sustaining vocalized sounds. Again, hissing is a controlled non-sound release. But when you sing, you are involving consonants and vowels and adding different levels of dynamics (how soft or loud the sound). This combination of dynamics applied to the consonants and vowels of your song can eat up the breath/fuel supply at a rapid rate.

The different mouth positions from vowels and consonants allow for more air to escape than a steady hiss. When vocalizing, you are working the vocal muscles, as opposed to hissing, which requires that the vocal cords remain uninvolved to allow the glottis to be wide open.

For this exercise, I want you to count out loud to ten as

many times as possible. Each time you reach ten, start over again, by beginning with the next highest number from one. For example:

1-2 3 4 5 6 7 8 9 10, 2-2 3 4 5 6 7 8 9 10 . . .
9-2 3 4 5 6 7 8 9 10, 10-2 3 4 5 6 7 8 9 10 . . .

Don't rush when you are counting. Keep it steady. A good rate would be one hundred twenty (120) beats per minute or two numbers per second. Rushing is cheating.

BREATH RELEASE #1 EXAMPLE

I made it through four sets of ten, so I'll write down the following:

BREATH RELEASE #1- 4X

BREATH RELEASE #2

The reason I had you count was to incorporate different vowels and consonants. As you recall from the last exercise, singing requires more air control than hissing, due to vocal cord involvement and different mouth positions.

This time, we are going to say our ABCs out loud, to cover all vowels and basic consonants. I know you aren't in kindergarten any more, but saying your ABCs is a great way to develop breath control. Again, like the last exercise, don't rush.

BREATH RELEASE #2 EXAMPLE

I made it through one full alphabet and to J, my second time through. When you fill in your chart, write down how many times you made it through the alphabet, and how far you made it into the next.

Since I made it through the alphabet one complete time and all the way to J in the second set, I'll write down the following:

BREATH RELEASE #2- 1-J

SUSTAIN #1

In the breath release exercises, we worked on increasing our sustain time. The first exercise in the program worked with controlled breath release through hissing.

The breath release exercises helped to develop breath release by "talking" your way through the alphabet and counting. But you are a singer, right? So shouldn't you be vocalizing when doing these exercises? Well, you are absolutely right! At this point in the program, it's time to start "vocalizing" (singing) while performing the exercises.

Since the whole point of this program is to develop breath control and to increase sustain time for singing, it only makes sense to vocalize for the last few exercises.

I want you to begin counting as high as you can while vocalizing. I want you to sustain a steady pitch while you count. I don't expect you to sing an opera while you count to one hundred, just maintain a steady even pitch as you count; a pitch that is comfortable for your current range, somewhere in the speaking voice level. You'll find that counting as you vocalize is a little tougher than counting to ten over and over again while only "speaking" the numbers. This is because singing requires more vocal cord "energy" creation as opposed to speaking.

SUSTAIN #1 EXAMPLE

I was only able to "vocalize" my way up to twenty my first time. Did you beat me? I hope so! While you fill in your chart, I'll write down the following:

SUSTAIN #1-2

SUSTAIN #2

I like to call this next exercise the buzzing exercise because it makes your head and chest "buzz" from resonance. Begin by sustaining a steady "zzzzzzz" until you can feel your whole head buzz.

When you become accustomed to the buzzing sensation on the "zzzzzzz", close your mouth and begin vocalizing an "mmmmmmm" sound. Set your stopwatch and sustain the "mmmmmmm" sound as long as you can.

Concentrate on creating a buzzing sensation in your head. You'll notice that your chest will possibly begin to "buzz" from the resonance as well.

The purpose of the "zzzzzzz" sound was to allow you to grow accustomed to the buzzing sensation that I want you to feel in your teeth, mouth, chest, and head, when sustaining the "mmmmmmm" sound. I mostly want you to focus on feeling this buzzing sensation in your teeth. The stronger the buzzing sensation you can produce against your teeth, the more resonance you are producing.

What is resonance? Resonance is the production of multiple sound waves when the sound of your voice "bounces around" in the open cavities of your body.

So basically, your voice reverberates inside your mouth, chest, throat, and skull, creating tons of echoes in your empty head. Haha, I'm just teasing about the empty head part. Actually resonance can occur throughout all of your body. You are your own reverb chamber; you are a human sized tuning fork!

Did I lose you? Still not sure what reverberate or resonance means? Let me clarify. Do you have any idea why your voice sounds so great in the shower? Because the sound waves produced by your voice are bouncing off the solid walls of the shower. This creates mini echoes of your voice (also known as reverberation), which in turn will make your voice sound fuller.

You can internally do the same by focusing on creating and increasing these mini echoes or reverberations. Focusing on a buzzing sensation in the teeth, cheeks, face and the entire body can easily and effortlessly reproduce multiple mini echoes, which enriches the sound quality and minimizes vocal stress by taking the weight of vocal production off of the vocal cords. Just mentally chant to yourself, "The better the buzz, the fuller voice" and you'll master this exercise (and improve your singing as well).

The cool thing is that the more reverberations, or resonance, you learn to produce, the less breath pressure you'll have to apply with your stomach in order to sustain a note. This is because the sound will build and float on the resonance, sort of like skipping a pebble on a pond produces wave after wave.

Here's another great mantra to chant to yourself: "Resonance will make the note "float" out of you". All right, back to the exercise. Turn on your stopwatch, start your zzzzzzz's. Then close your mouth and begin to sing "mmmmmm" for as long as you can.

Concentrate on keeping the teeth buzzing regardless of pitch. If it's a low pitch, try to get your chest buzzing as well as your teeth. When you practice on higher pitches, try to feel the buzzing in your head. You might even get a little dizzy from the buzzing in your head. That's all right. This means you are doing great.

SUSTAIN #2 EXAMPLE

So how did you do? Don't forget to write down your time. I'll bet you held out longer than I did. I made it to forty seconds. So I'll write down the following:

SUSTAIN #2- 40 SECONDS

SUSTAIN #3

This last exercise is my favorite. In fact, this is what I used to do before I knew anything about breathing exercises. It is also the basis of breath control that I use for the *Raise Your Voice* system. This one exercise will produce dramatic results, but the whole system will make you a breathing superstar.

It's very simple. All I want you to do is sing and sustain an "A" vowel, like in "play", for as long as you possibly can. Start on a pitch that is comfortable for your range. I don't want you to strain. You should continue to use the pitch you have chosen for several weeks, or until you can sustain that pitch for at least thirty seconds.

SUSTAIN #3 EXAMPLE

After you have mastered your first initial pitch, continue working your way up the scale a half step at a time until you can hold each pitch in your range for at least thirty seconds. So if you start on an E below **Tenor C**, move up to an F after you can hold the E for thirty seconds.

When you can hold the F for thirty seconds, move up to an F#, G, G# and so on and so forth. . . .

When you have covered your entire range, start from the bottom again, only this time change your sustain time to forty seconds. Each time you have mastered your range, start again from the bottom with a five to ten second increase in sustain time as your new goal.

Also I should note that I do not want you using this exercise for range increase. Just go as high as you feel that you can comfortably sustain a note without straining to maintain that note.

Do you remember in the beginning of the book when I told you about how I am always asked about how I am able to hold out notes for long periods at a time? This particular exercise is basically what I am doing when I sustain long notes. I hold out a pitch, like a **Tenor C** for as long as I can, using the secrets from the next chapter. When performing live, I've held out notes for right over a minute.

Back to the exercise: I sang an E below **Tenor C** for twenty-five seconds. Maybe tomorrow I'll hit thirty seconds and move

44

on to an F. So while you fill in your chart, I'll write down both the note and the length that I held the note:

SUSTAIN #3- E/25 SECONDS

This completes the basic nine-step exercise program. Keep your diary daily and watch your progress soar. To further your progress and assure developing the best breathing machine possible, let's move onto some breathing secrets:

THE SECRETS

Now *that you have mastered* the exercises, (I know you've been practicing day and night, right?), I want to share with you some breathing secrets that will make you a breathing superstar. Okay, maybe I lied. If you've read my first book *Raise Your Voice*, then you know the #1 major secret. I can sum it up in one sentence: Pretend you are inhaling (breathing in) while you are singing (breathing out). I call this the **Inhalation Sensation**.

Before I explain this secret in detail, I have a few others that I need to discuss with you first. These secrets will prove that breathing is an essential part of singing.

Most of these secrets aren't really secrets at all. They are just common sense breath technique applications that some people just don't know about. We have already covered several of these secrets throughout the book, but I believe that they should be reviewed.

You should begin applying these secrets to your exercise routine and using them each and every time you breathe, talk, and sing.

THE FIRST SECRET:
DIAPHRAGMATIC/LOWER ABDOMINAL BREATHING
Years ago, before I developed my vocal range, I was singing in a cover band and I was having trouble singing the **Kansas** tune "**Carry On, Wayward Son**". The only way I was able to sing

the song without straining was by practicing a new breathing technique I had learned that required me to expand my stomach.

Although I didn't fully understand the term "diaphragmatic breathing" at that time, I was still reaping the benefits of correct breath technique. Wow, imagine that, proper breath technique can eliminate vocal strain! If you aren't pushing as hard and wasting away your air supply, your vocal cords won't be over-stressed, and your voice will benefit.

Although diaphragmatic (belly breathing) is the first secret, it doesn't stop there.

THE SECOND SECRET:
KEEPING YOUR RIBS EXPANDED!

If you keep the ribs expanded as you sing and release your breath, you help to maintain an open chest cavity, and keep the diaphragm down. This gives your lungs "room to breathe", so to speak, and slows breath release. An expanded ribcage will give you a bigger sound and will minimize vocal stress. An expanded belly helped me to defeat **Kansas**, but, by keeping my ribs expanded, I was able to conquer **Judas Priest**.

Let's Combine the First Two Secrets Together For the

THIRD SECRET:
MAXIMUM BREATH POTENTIAL!

This type of breathing combines both chest and diaphragmatic breathing, for full lung capacity. Fill your lungs from the bottom up, expanding your stomach below the navel first, then the back, ribs then chest, and . . . always keep your ribs expanded!

Remember; you don't need to take a huge breath to sustain long notes. It's about controlling the release of the breath. You can still expand all these areas without a huge gulp of air. Heck, I can expand my ribs without even taking a breath. The point is that you need to expand them for more room for resonance expansion. If you are still having a little trouble, the next few secrets will help.

THE FOURTH SECRET:
THE CREATION OF RESONANCE

Resonance plays a major role in sound quality, vocal freedom and effortless breath control. A guide to creating maximum resonance is to always maintain the sensation of buzzing in your teeth when you sing. If you can do this while you sing, you will be able to create resonance within the body and the notes will float out with little breath effort.

This doesn't undermine the importance of chest and head resonance. The buzzing sensation in the teeth is a sure sign that both head and chest resonance are present. A little trick to get more buzz out of the teeth is by focusing the sound of your voice up into the roof of the mouth also known as the palate. If you feel a buzzing in the roof of your mouth simultaneously with the buzzing of the teeth, you are onto something special called vocal placement. If you want to know more about resonance production and vocal placement, check out my book *Raise Your Voice*.

THE FIFTH SECRET:
LEARNING TO CORRECTLY INHALE AND EXHALE

It might sound silly, but many people do not know how to

inhale and exhale properly. The majority of vocal problems stem from inhalation and exhalation.

When you inhale, you want to maintain a quiet almost completely silent breath. You accomplish this by keeping the vocal cords wide open. How do you keep the cords open? Take a big yawn. If you hear any breathiness as you inhale, you aren't opening the vocal cords wide enough to allow free release because you are introducing vocal cord resistance. You are keeping the cords together, which is drying them out. The cords must stay lubricated to vibrate properly. Play around with a big yawn until the breath is almost silent.

Unnecessarily drying out the vocal cords only endangers vocal health. The best way for singers to inhale the breath is to keep the ribs expanded before you inhale, and to incorporate what I call a micro-quiet breath on a slight yawn. That is why I just had you practicing the quiet breath on a yawn. The micro-breath is a very quick breath that you should barely be able to hear. The slight yawn opens up the throat for unobstructed inhaling and exhaling.

INHALATION EXAMPLE

Exhaling can be as damaging as inhaling. If you sound breathy, or like **Darth Vader**, when you exhale, (or even when you inhale) you can be sure that you are breathing incorrectly. Focus on eliminating this habit.

EXHALATION EXAMPLE.

Okay . . . finally, we're back to the **Inhalation Sensation.** . . .

THE SIXTH SECRET:
THE #1 MAJOR SECRET TO SUSTAINING NOTES AND GAINING
BREATH CONTROL – THE INHALATION SENSATION

When I first discovered this technique (on my own) I was utilizing my **Maximum Breath Potential**. I was applying lower abdominal breathing. When I would sing, I would expand my ribs and take a deep belly breath all the way down below my navel. I was also working on resonance by keeping my teeth buzzing and focusing my sound into my palate. When I first discovered the **Inhalation Sensation**, I was able to double my sustain time with ease that very same day!

I really don't even remember how it happened, but it worked wonders! I was performing live and I remember having to hold out a really long note. I was about halfway through the note and felt like I was almost out of breath. I thought I was going to have to give up and I wasn't going to be able to hold out any longer. . . . All of a sudden my whole mental and vocal setup switched gears. . . .

Suddenly, it felt like I was breathing in the note as I was singing. I felt like I wasn't exhaling anymore and the note was effortlessly floating right out of me! So, I kept holding and holding and holding the note out until everyone, including myself, was in a state of total disbelief. Not only did I hold the note as long as I needed, I kept going! I held the note out almost three times as long as I had to. Thus the **Inhalation Sensation** was born. From that day on I have applied the **Inhalation Sensation** technique to my singing exercises, to my breathing exercises and to my vocal performances.

I believe the reason the **Inhalation Sensation** works is because when you visualize inhaling as opposed to exhaling, you actually release any excess or incorrect stomach muscle tension (like when grunting) that is applied up towards the diaphragm.

This simple mental trick helps to keep the diaphragm down and allows the diaphragm to relax at a natural rate, which in turn slows the air release from the lungs. This technique is an added bonus and an aid to your **Maximum Breath Potential**.

Start applying the **Inhalation Sensation** to all of your breathing exercises immediately. Make sure to note in your diary the day you started using this technique. I bet you'll start noticing a huge difference in your sustains immediately.

THE SEVENTH AND FINAL SECRET:
CORRECTLY TIGHTENING THE STOMACH MUSCLES FOR
BREATH CONTROL AND POWER – THE POWER PUSH

This "secret" has been used by most of the big rock stars of the 80's and has increased range and power through a simple application of the stomach muscles. . . .

Remember when I said that you should never lock the stomach or throat? This is still totally true, but. . . . Do you remember when I said there was a correct way to tighten the stomach? What if I told you there were a way to tighten the stomach that would actually give you more power, volume, and range, while helping to eliminate unnecessary breath pressure?

Eighty-six year old Californian voice teacher and author of *Strengthening Your Singing Voice*, **Elizabeth Sabine** has one of the biggest, strongest voices I've ever heard, and she's no bigger than a minute! She has taught singers like **Axl Rose** of **Guns N' Roses** and **Don Barnes** of **38 Special** and was considered one of the best-kept secrets of the music industry. None of her huge list of clients wanted any of their vocal competition knowing what they had learned from her.

While preparing for my appearance on the **Discovery Channel** show **MythBusters**, I was having trouble breaking wine glasses with my voice, without amplification (who wouldn't have trouble with that). Then I read **Elizabeth Sabine's** book, *Strengthening Your Singing Voice*, and started applying her techniques. My voice seemed to become louder and stronger, in only a few minutes, if that's possible. It gave me that little extra kick of power that I needed to break the glasses and as of right now, I have broken too many to count.

Needless to say, I started analyzing my vocal technique and realized that I had unconsciously been doing the same thing on high notes for years but didn't know it. Right then I realized that by developing and focusing on this unusual technique, I could improve my voice. I talked to a friend of mine, **Jim Gillette**, and he told me that he always tightened down his stomach muscles to hit those "banshee" screams with his band **Nitro**.

One of my favorite singers, **Josey Scott**, of **Saliva**, told me that he always feels as if he sings from his stomach area.

Elizabeth claims that volume and power should come from the diaphragm, abdominal and back muscles, not the vocal cords. She likens the diaphragm to a big speaker cone. If you engage the stomach muscles correctly, you create electrical energy that powers the speaker cone.

To activate this electrical energy, all you need to do is tighten the stomach muscles by pushing straight down, just like going to the bathroom, sneezing or childbirth. This is the only correct way to create the electrical energy needed to power the diaphragm.

If you tighten the stomach muscles any other way for this technique, you are doing it wrong. You cannot lock the muscles like when grunting. This will lock up the vocal cords, preventing airflow and causing vocal strain. You also should not force the stomach straight out or suck the stomach in for support. Only by supporting down will you increase vocal power. So to sum it up; tightening up, out or in does not relieve excess breath pressure. **Only tighten straight down!**

To properly use your diaphragm for this technique, you must keep the ribs expanded, but you should be doing this out of habit by now. This allows the diaphragm to lay down flat and very wide, like a speaker cone.

It helps to visualize the sound coming straight out at diaphragm level and right up into your palate as you sing to keep the pressure off the vocal cords. So with ribs wide and the stomach tightened straight down, try singing up into the palate from your diaphragm and see if this method works for you. On low notes, the ribs will be expanded wide and on higher notes the ribs will come in some and the diaphragm will rise slightly to a point.

If you want more range, volume, power, or want to sing with some grit added to your voice, then you MUST master this secret! Psst. . . . I call this secret the **Power Push.**

If done correctly, you can never over-do it. The downward stomach pressure helps to keep the diaphragm down and the air pressure off the vocal cords. The tighter you push down, the more electricity you produce, the less air pressure on the cords and the louder, stronger, and higher you will be able to sing.

Elizabeth also says that you must also become very passionate about your singing, crying out with emotion as you sing every line. Do you remember when you were a child and you shouted, "I DON'T WANT TO GO TO SCHOOL!"? Do you remember that intensity and passion in your voice? I bet you never lost your voice at that tender age. That's because you tightened your stomach as you shouted with passion and conviction. If you intend to be a great singer, you must be passionate when you sing. **Lajon Witherspoon** of **Sevendust** once told me that you have to sing with passion and conviction if you want to make it as a singer.

SHOUTING DEMONSTRATION

Elizabeth's book, *Strengthening Your Singing Voice*, is a must-read. To learn more about **Elizabeth Sabine** and her teaching methods, check out her website www.elizabethsabine.net.

So once more I'll explain the entire breathing process:

1. With the ribs expanded, take a micro-breath on a yawn to begin filling the lungs from the bottom-up, while focusing on expanding the stomach below the navel. This is what I call your **Maximum Breath Potential.**

2. When you begin to sing, make sure that you **keep your ribs expanded!** The intercostals will oppose the stomach muscles to fight for control of the air release rate from the lungs. Don't forget to keep a downward tension in your stomach and back muscles, like blowing out a candle. It's an opposing process. And, if you want more power, tighten the stomach muscles

straight down, like going to the bathroom.

3. Resonance production in the body will help the notes to "float" right out of you effortlessly. You should develop resonance within the whole body, not just the teeth. Always focus the sound up into the palate and maintain a buzzing sensation in the teeth. For a more detailed explanation of full resonance expansion, read *Raise Your Voice*. You can purchase *Raise Your Voice* (actually it's *Raise Your Voice: Second Edition*) at my website www.raiseyourvoicebook.com.

4. Utilize the **Inhalation Sensation**. Just pretend that you are inhaling instead of exhaling when you sing. This will make the job of the diaphragm and intercostals easier. You'll double your sustain time!

5. Singing with lots of passion and conviction. This will give you a stronger, more believable voice, with less of a chance of losing your voice. When you sing with emotion, you'll tighten the stomach muscles down (Power Push) and take the strain of excess breath pressure off your vocal cords.

That's it! You now possess the knowledge that will enable you to compete in the Breathing Olympics. It's up to you now. Only you can make this happen. Try this program for at least one month. If you try this program for three months, you'll be amazed at the progress you've made! In the next chapter, I'll share with you *my* actual "breathing diary" that I created during the conception of this program back in 1990.

THE CHART

12/03 1990	A.R. #1	A.R. #2	B.C. #1	B.C. #2	B.R. #1	B.R. #2	S. #1	S. #2	S. #3
12/03	31 sec	2X	44 sec	25 sec	4X	1-J	20	40 sec	E/25 sec
12/04	32 sec	2X	45 sec	26 sec	4X	1-L	21	40 sec	E/25 sec
12/05	35 sec	2X	46 sec	27 sec	4X	1-M	22	40 sec	E/27 sec
12/06	36 sec	3X	47 sec	28 sec	4X	1-N	23	41 sec	E/28 sec
12/07	37 sec	3X	48 sec	29 sec	5X	1-T	23	42 sec	E/29 sec
12/08	38 sec	3X	49 sec	30 sec	5X	1-U	24	43 sec	E/30 sec
12/09	39 sec	3X	50 sec	31 sec	5X	1-V	25	43 sec	F/14 sec
12/10	41 sec	3X	55 sec	32 sec	5X	2	27	45 sec	F/15 sec
12/11	41 sec	3X	56 sec	33 sec	5X	2	30	45 sec	F/17 sec
12/12	42 sec	3X	57 sec	34 sec	6X	2-D	31	45 sec	F/20 sec

12/13	43 sec	3X	58 sec	35 sec	6X	2-E	32	47 sec	F/22 sec
12/14	44 sec	4X	1 min	36 sec	6X	2-E	35	47 sec	F/23 sec
12/15	45 sec	4X	1 min	37 sec	6X	2-G	38	48 sec	F/24 sec
12/16	47 sec	4X	61 sec	38 sec	7X	2-H	40	49 sec	F/25 sec
12/17	48 sec	4X	62 sec	39 sec	7X	2-I	41	50 sec	F/25 sec
12/18	49 sec	4X	63 sec	40 sec	7X	2-J	42	51 sec	F/28 sec
12/19	50 sec	4X	67 sec	41 sec	7X	2-K	44	52 sec	F/30 sec
12/20	51 sec	4X	68 sec	42 sec	7X	2-N	45	52 sec	F#/16 sec
12/21	52 sec	4X	68 sec	43 sec	7X	2-O	47	54 sec	F#/16 sec
12/22	54 sec	4X	70 sec	44 sec	8X	2-Q	52	55 sec	F#/19 sec
12/23	55 sec	5X	70 sec	47 sec	8X	2-S	55	56 sec	F#/20 sec
12/24	56 sec	5X	70 sec	48 sec	8X	2-U	58	57 sec	F#/20 sec
12/25	57 sec	5X	74 sec	51 sec	8X	2-W	59	1 min	F#/22 sec
12/26	58 sec	5X	75 sec	54 sec	8X	2-Y	64	61 sec	F#/23 sec

12/27	59 sec	5X	77 sec	56 sec	9X	3	66	62 sec	F#/24 sec
12/28	59 sec	5X	80 sec	58 sec	9X	3	70	63 sec	F#/25 sec
12/29	64 sec	5X	82 sec	1 min	9X	3-A	70	64 sec	F#/25 sec
12/30	67 sec	5X	85 sec	1 min	11X	3-B	74	65 sec	F#/25 sec

On the previous pages, I've presented to you a four-week chart of my actual "breathing diary" from the conception of this unique program back in 1990. It's pretty simple to follow. You should know how to fill out the chart by now; that is, if you were keeping track of your progress on a sheet of paper as we learned the exercises. A chart just makes it simpler to track your progress. When you make your chart, be sure to fill out the date you began the program in the top left corner, like I did. Keep track of the date every day. If you don't want to make your own chart and prefer a diary for singers, check out my book *The Ultimate Vocal Workout Diary*.

If you review the chart, you'll notice that I steadily improved every week. Although my gains were not dramatic, I did continue increasing my sustain times. I would strive each day to increase all the exercises by at least one second, one number or one letter. I knew that if I could reach forty seconds one day, then I should be able to reach forty-one seconds the next. If I didn't reach my goal, I didn't get discouraged. You'll find that in the beginning, you increase your numbers by leaps and bounds. Then, you might go through a slow process of increasing sustain times. Don't worry; this is normal.

If you want to reach your breathing potential, you should do this program for three months straight as I did. I could have put my three-month chart in the book, but I figured four weeks would be more than enough to explain the program. I still want you to aim for three months. Strive for at least one more second, number, or letter each day.

To be an excellent singer takes more than correct breath technique. You need guidance in improving your singing voice. Some great books and methods are Jim Gillette's *Vocal Power*, Thomas Appell's, *Can You Sing a High C Without Straining?*, Brett Manning's *Singing Success* Program, Melissa Cross' *Zen of Screaming*, Robert Lunte's *The Four Pillars of Singing*, Mark Baxter's *Rock-n-Roll Singer's Survival Manual*, and Elizabeth Sabine's *Strengthening Your Singing Voice*, as well as my book, *Raise Your Voice: Second Edition*. You can learn about these teachers on Google and you can purchase many of these products through jaimevendera.com, elizabethsabine.net and the rockdoctors.net. So how did I do at the end of three months compared to my first day?

FIRST DAY

Abdominal Release #1- 31 seconds
Abdominal Release #2- 2X
Breath Capacity #1- 44 seconds
Breath Capacity #2- 25 seconds
Breath Release #1- 4X
Breath Release #2- 1-J
Sustain #1- 20

Sustain #2- 40 seconds
Sustain #3- E/25 seconds

AFTER FOUR WEEKS

Abdominal Release #1- 67 seconds
Abdominal Release #2- 5X
Breath Capacity #1- 85 seconds
Breath Capacity #2- 1 minute
Breath Release #1- 11X
Breath Release #2- 3-B
Sustain #1- 74
Sustain #2- 65 seconds
Sustain #3- F#/25 seconds

AFTER THREE MONTHS

Abdominal Release #1- 122 seconds
Abdominal Release #2- 12X
Breath Capacity #1- 4 minutes-15 seconds
Breath Capacity #2- 3 minutes
Breath Release #1- 21x
Breath Release #2- 7-R
Sustain #1-154
Sustain #2- 1 minute-22 seconds
Sustain #3- G/1 minute-10 seconds

If you want gains like mine, you must dedicate yourself completely to practicing this program. Only then will you see dramatic results like these. Good luck. Only you can decide your outcome with this program. Only you can make your own luck by practicing! So, what are you waiting for? I'm done talking. Get busy!

For Advanced Breathers

Whoops; wait a minute. I thought I was done jabbering. Guess I was wrong. Here are a few "breathing bonuses" for all of you air addicts. The following exercises are NOT part of the regular routine, but can and should be added as suggested. I consider these exercises for the advanced breather . . . if you aren't scared.

BREATH BUILDERS

I'd like to share with you what I call the "Breath Builders". They are an excellent way to build the stomach, back, diaphragmatic and intercostal muscles as well as expand the lungs. I learned a neat little trick to strengthen the lungs one day when I was hurriedly trying to fill up an air mattress as fast as I could. (Tony, remember?)

Being the crazy person I am, I figured out how to turn it into an exercise. Being that I am advanced breather, I figured that I better break it down into easier steps before I had any student tackle an air mattress. So now that you kind of have an idea of where I am going, let me get you started.

BREATH BUILDER #1

There are three different exercises in the Breath Builder series and the first exercise is performed with a simple balloon. Get a nice size balloon, one that will really expand. Simply blow it up repeatedly as many times as you can before you get light-headed. If you want to make it exciting, volunteer to blow up several hundred balloons for a party. Try this exercise at least three days a week for a few weeks.

No I don't mean keep volunteering for balloon blowing at parties three times a week. That was a one-time suggestion. Strive to blow up one balloon as many times as you can in one session, or blow up as many balloons as you can and then give them to you kid brother or sister to play with. In a couple of weeks when you feel you've mastered this exercise and are ready for a better challenge, move on to the second exercise.

BREATH BUILDER #2

Well, I hope it is summer while you are reading this because you are going to need a small blowup floating raft; the kind for pool lounging, and it might be hard to find one in the winter . . . unless you live in Florida.

Once you have your raft, set your stopwatch (yes you'll need your stopwatch for this exercise) and see just how fast you can completely blow it up. If you've been doing your regular daily routine, I bet you'll surprise yourself at how fast you can accomplish this task.

After a few weeks and once you've become accustomed to this exercise, move on to the third exercise.

BREATH BUILDER #3

Ah, last but not least, the initial reason a light went off in my head to create this series of exercises. I was visiting a close friend of mine and had to blow up an air mattress. Luckily for me, I didn't have an air pump. Yeah most people would have griped and complained but I took it as a personal challenge to prove just how strong my lungs were. Well, I impressed my friend (you know who you are, brother) and myself and blew it up in under a half hour. I believe it was closer to less than twenty minutes, but don't quote me on that.

So, for this exercise you'll need to purchase one of those blue full size air mattresses. Set your timer and go to work. Your goal is to beat me. I'm going to stick to my "right under twenty minutes" story to make you work harder.

At this point, I'd like to offer a word of caution. If you get light headed, stop and take a break. Beating me isn't worth passing out. You are taking in a lot more oxygen then you are used to, unless of course you do a lot of cardio regularly.

Be patient. The more you do this last exercise, the stronger your lungs, intercostals, stomach muscles, back muscles and diaphragm will become and it will become easier and quicker for you to do. I only suggest trying this exercise once a week.

The Breath Builder series truly are a series of breath building exercises; they are meant to be complimentary exercises to your regular routine and will dramatically increase your regular routine gains.

If keeping a balloon, pool float and inflatable bed in your home isn't convenient; you might want to check out the PTD-1 breath trainer.

The PTD-1 breath trainer is one of the more interesting means of locating and training the muscles utilized for correct breathing. The PTD-1 allows you to easily isolate the muscles involved in the inhalation and exhalation process. By focusing upon the muscles, you can speed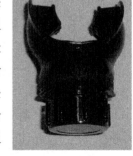

up the learning process regarding which muscles you must use when expanding your ribs and maintaining an 'open' chest cavity.

The PTD-1 features a hypoallergenic synthetic rubber mouthpiece and an adjustable compressions valve to control the flow of air in both directions through the trainer. This has the advantage over the breath builders of allowing you to train on both the inhalation and exhalation process. There are similar devices on the market, but none of them feature a program specifically designed by a vocalist for vocalists. For more information regarding the PTD-1 go to www. vocalistsdirect.com or you can purchase it through my site, www.thevoiceconnection.com or directly through www. rocksource360.com.

Here are some other amazing options for strengthening the core of your breath support; your abdominal muscles:

APPLIED BREATHING ISOMETRICS

Here is another intensive breath bonus for you breathing fanatics that I dubbed "Applied Breathing Isometrics" This series of exercises is guaranteed to get your heart pumping, your energy skyrocketing, your metabolism jumping and might even make you lose a few pounds. Applied Breathing Isometrics (ABI for short) are exercises designed to work on building the abs while also increasing oxygen intake. So without further ado, here is the first exercise:

ABI EXERCISE #1-POWER PANTS

No, I am not talking about your jeans; I am talking about panting like a dog. This exercise is so intense that, for your safety, you should sit down when performing this one. All you have to do is pant like crazy in a precise order/rhythm. Since I already know you can count from the earlier exercises, haha, we are going to mentally count for this exercise. So the order is this:

> Pant ten times. . . . Pause
> Pant twenty times. . . . Pause, etc. . . .

All you basically do is begin by panting as fast as you can to a count of ten, take a small break, then begin panting again, adding ten reps each time you perform the routine. So in other words you will pause for a few second in between panting and the numbers should go like 10, 20, 30, 40, 50. . . .

Try at first by working up to fifty. If you make it to fifty, you will have panted one hundred fifty times. That is a lot of oxygen intake in a short amount of time. This is cardio for the lazy person, like me, haha. I currently use this in the morning and work to one hundred but I have gone much higher. Don't over do it, I don't want you passing out.

ABI EXERCISE #2-CARDIO SINGING

Cardio singing is a concept I recently adopted that I believe should be adopted by every singer! Simply put, vocalize as you run, jog, bike, jump on a rebounder or do aerobics. (I would've added swimming, but that might be a little tough with all the water.) That's all there is to it. Well really it is a lot harder than it sounds. This is something you will have to build up to in stamina. It has the added bonus of helping you develop vocal stamina for singing long sets at a gig.

My idea of cardio singing is jogging and power walking. I personally have an hour of music on my mp3 player that I listen to over and over again as I run/walk. In the beginning, I listened, and then hummed along to the tunes as I ran. In time I was able to begin singing along at a low volume.

The key is mastering your breath control during cardio because cardio newbies have a tendency to begin taking very shallow, fast breaths as they become tired. This will turn you into a chest breather faster than I could ever say "cardio diaphragmatic propelled upper chest breathing overload". You want to maintain a deep, slow, controlled breath in order to not get overheated or allow your breathing to become shallow. If jogging is too hard on your knees, try jogging on a rebounder. Now onto the last exercise:

ABI EXERCISE #3-THREE MINUTE WORKOUT

Yes that is correct, this exercise will only take three minutes to perform! Just follow the following three-minute process.

1ST MINUTE

Pant, pant, pant, just like in the "Extreme Breathing Exercise" from my book *Raise Your Voice*. The goal is to flood the body with oxygen. You might get a bit light headed, feel flushed or slightly warmer, but this is normal. This is due to the rush of oxygen into the bloodstream and to the brain. This is a good thing because it boosts your energy levels. Now, with that said, DO NOT perform this exercise (or any other in this book) while driving or operating equipment. Find a comfortable place to stand, sit or lie down. Once that minute is up, quit panting; relax for several seconds, then take several slow, deep breaths, before moving on.

2ND MINUTE

Inhale from the bottom up, to complete capacity and then hold your breath. DO NOT lock the breath at your throat! You should effortlessly be able to maintain full breath capacity by keeping the floating ribs expanded to your sides while still focusing in an inhalation sensation.

Once you are completely full, start your timer and begin a series of 'micro pants', or tiny inhales to expand the back, stomach and intercostals outwards and diaphragm down. You might be saying "but I am already full." Not to worry because small amounts of air will escape from the lungs as you do this because of the body's ability to equalize the air pressure. Just refill on the micro pant in a continual minute long fluid movement. The goal of this minute is to stretch and relax all of the muscles involved in breath support. Once the minute is up, relax and take several deep breaths before moving on.

3RD MINUTE

Now we've relaxed our breathing machine, let's do some strengthening. This time I want you to completely exhale to the point that the stomach caves inwards. Once empty, start your timer and focus on a continual minute long flow of micro breath releases. It's works better if you focus on bringing the stomach in and up as you do this. This lung/vacuum approach will allow small amounts of air to creep back in order to equalize pressure. The goal is to strengthen the inner core; or inner band of stomach muscles and back muscles.

If you are doing a cardio or yoga program like FlowFit® (as

mentioned in *Raise Your Voice: Second Edition*) this is great exercise to add in with that routine. Another routine singers should adopt is some form of abdominal training for vocal power. My choice is Be Breathed®, which is another part of the FlowFit® family; a Vocal-Flow system for singers (vocal-flow.com) I'll let my friend Ryan Murdock tell you about it:

BE BREATHED®

My name is Ryan Murdock. I'm a faculty coach for RMAX International (creators of the Circular Strength Training® system) as well as a widely published travel writer/explorer. As a coach, I work with a wide variety of rock stars, including **Nitro's Jim Gillette**, guitar Diva **Lita Ford** and **Steve Kilbey** of Australian legends **The Church.**

In working with these high-octane performers at the peak of their craft, I've learned that core strength and breath control are absolutely crucial for both vocalization and stage performance. The progressions in the Be Breathed® system **always** form the introduction to core work for my clients.

To perform at your best, your breathing must be integrated. Be Breathed® is a foundational program for training total breath integration and core strength through a full range of motion.

Be Breathed® will teach you to use your body as a bellows as you seamlessly integrate your breathing, structure and movement-"being breathed" in the most effortlessly way possible. You'll bring new meaning to the term 'washboard abs' by **throttling your core with just ten repetitions,** and you'll never waste your time with sit-ups or crunches again. You'll also learn the trademark CST method of Perpetual

Exercise, which will allow you to squeeze in a few reps while driving your car, watching television, or sitting in the green room. What does this mean for singers and musicians?

- Be Breathed is *the* system for developing the breath support mechanism.
- Be Breathed strengthens the abdominals, intercostals, and back muscles, all of which are crucial to the development of breath support and a powerful vocal delivery
- Be Breathed helps vocalists develop a concise breathing pattern, thus minimizing breath pressure and vocal stress during singing

Be Breathed® relaxes the mind and body. Continual practice of the program will allow you to take that relaxation to the stage, clearing your mind of performance anxiety and minimizing bodily tension for a better live performance and greater vocal stamina.

Like FlowFit®, the Be Breathed® program is structured incrementally. It's accessible to beginners but it's also capable of kicking the butt of the most elite athlete. As Jaime Vendera is so fond of saying, singers and musicians are athletes too—but they don't have the luxury of all day training sessions. If you want to **get your abs on in less than 10 minutes per day**, this program is for you.

(Coach Murdock also offers a line of affordable, down-loadable training tutorials. Each download is a complete stand-alone program, and is accessible to anyone regardless of fitness level. 'Beyond Situps' contains the basic template of the Be Breathed® program, and takes it to new heights of movement sophistication. Visit his site to purchase any of these programs today at: http://www.rmaxstaff.com/murdock/products.html)

Note: With the exception of Be Breathed®, these advanced exercises are not necessarily routines you need to adopt as part of your regular Ultimate Breathing Workout routine. Be Breathed® is the wise choice for developing the abdominal muscles and I suggest you use it in place of any sit-up routine you are currently using. The advanced exercises from this chapter were designed to give you options for further strength training. If you decide to add any of these routines, you should write down your gains every time you do these exercises and keep track of you progress.

So now I guess it IS really time to get busy. Have fun with Ultimate Breathing Workout and don't forget to stop by The Voice Connection Message Forum and tell us about your results.

If you've become a breathing addict and want to change your breath to change your life, I also suggest that you stop by several sites like breathing.com, jaimevendera.com and the rockdoctors.net to learn more about breathing.

Now if you don't mind, I've got an air mattress to blow up.

THE END

I *knew this part would* eventually come. I hope that you have enjoyed *The Ultimate Breathing Workout* and I hope that you have learned a lot about your breathing habits. If you weren't a champion breather, I believe that you are now.

The Ultimate Breathing Workout is the perfect companion manual to my first book, *Raise Your Voice*, the owner's manual for the voice. If you practice the techniques from both books you'll be able to hit notes as high and hold notes as long as **this singer. (audio file)**

Wow! That was pretty amazing! This incredible 32-second scream was from a song called **Machine Gunn Eddie**. The singer was none other than my friend, mentor and vocal coach, **Jim Gillette** of **Nitro**. Of course, **Jim** would say that if you are going to hit notes that high and hold em' for that long, you'd better practice, practice, practice. So, get busy! See ya next book!

ABOUT THE AUTHOR

World-renowned glass shattering vocal coach, **Jaime Vendera** has studied voice for more than twenty years. He started singing at the age of three when he discovered the power  that the voice gave him to become the center of attention.

Jaime's early life was enriched in the fine arts, including instrumental studies of saxophone, flute, harmonica and piano, singing in school & college choir, and performing in theatrical arts.

Singing professionally since the age of sixteen, **Jaime** didn't begin studying voice until the age of eighteen when he felt he could go no further without fully understanding the concepts of true vocal production, stage performance and the functioning of both the singing and speaking voice.

After a year of vocal study under the guidance of vocal instructor **Shirley Crothers**, at **Shawnee State University** in Ohio, **Jaime** moved to Hollywood, California to study voice at the **Vocal Institute of Technology** at the **Musician's Institute**.

Still yearning for a deeper understanding of voice, he also studied vocal and health related subjects such as vocal and breathing technique, yoga, reflexology, herbology, and hypnosis. Still yearning for more, he sought out the advice of professionals such as **Jim Gillette** and **Tony Harnell** among others as well as vocal coaches such as, **Thomas Appell, James Carson, Elizabeth Sabine** and **Mark Baxter.**

After extensive years of training and studying voice, **Jaime** has authored several books, training CDs, vocal health products and a software program for singers.

With the aid and guidance of one of **Jaime's** top vocal coaches, **Jim Gillette, Jaime** perfected the art of shattering glass with his voice, and has appeared on **Good Morning America**, as a guest of **Jamie Hyneman** and **Adam Savage** of the **Discovery Channel** hit, **MythBusters**, shattering a wine glass, with the aid of an amplifier.

His **GMA** success led to his appearance on **MythBusters**, where he set a world record, confirming that a singer can shatter a glass with the un-amplified voice, leading to a multitude of television shows worldwide. **Jaime** is officially the first documented singer on film to shatter a glass by voice alone.

Jaime is currently and continually working on methods to improve vocal production including new books, DVDs, voice related products and seminars.

Jaime, Michael, Ben Carrol and **Greg Pettis** have come together to create rocksource360.com; a company dedicated to creating a community for consulting and training rock musicians (guitarists, bass players, drummers, keyboard wizards, singers, managers, roadies, engineers, etc) in order to help avid artists perfect their techniques to their fullest potential.

Besides being a workaholic, **Jaime** spends time with his family. **Jaime**, along with his wife, **Diane**, their son **Ryan**, their two Chihuahuas **Taco** and **Belle**, and their Dachshunds **Axl** and **Miley** currently reside in Ohio.

THANKS

I *would like to thank God* and the Lord Jesus Christ for always filling my heart with ideas. I can't turn it off and that's not a bad thing. To my loving wife Diane; this book didn't take as long as the last. To my son Ryan; the best bass player in the world. To the three men who made it possible for me to regain my vocal chops after surgery; Tim Odle, Greg Seymour, and Joe Conley. To Daniel Middleton; thanks for all of your help and guidance; I'm glad we partnered up. To Molly Burnside; how do you put up with me? To Amy Chesbro; thank you for making me a better writer. To Benoit Guerville; for all you do for me; Your amazing vision keeps me inspired. To all of the singer's and vocal coaches that I have interviewed thus far at The Voice Connection; without you, I wouldn't have a website. To Elizabeth Sabine; thank you for strengthening my singing voice. Extra special thanks to Jim Gillette; Where do I start . . . Thank you so much for teaching me to shatter glass, getting me on national television, allowing me to use a sound clip of your incredible voice for this book, calling me up and playing all of your new material over the phone, not making fun of me when I sang your songs to you, haha, believing in me and the website, and most of all . . . being a great friend! To Tony Harnell; you know these updates were because of the pep-talk you gave me in the café' the last time I visited. You helped to finely tune my vision and I thank you for it. You really are my brother; even 'mom' knows it. To Pam Anders; you've showed me that breathing can be a real trip . . . Literally! To my three RockDoctor brothers, Ben Carroll, Greg Pettis and Michael Rocchio; without your support and vision, the RockDoctors would still be a thought in our heads. Thanks for putting up to me when I'm cranky. Finally, to all of my Voice Connection fans and *Raise Your Voice* students: You are the reason that I keep exploring the concepts of voice.

God bless,

Jaime Vendera

NOTES

NOTES

CPSIA information can be obtained at www.ICGtesting.com
Printed in the USA
BVOW09s2040111114

374654BV00025B/624/P

9 780974 941141